Moyle Memories
- 50 years and beyond.

An album of memories from around the District of Moyle.

Written by Danny McGill.

Edited by Tommy McDonald.

Acknowledgements

Published in 2008 by Impact Printing.

*Written by Daniel.J.McGill. B.Sc. Nationwide Community and Heritage Awards Regional Winner 2008.
Edited by Tommy McDonald.*

Funded by the McCaughan Group.

© Copyright Daniel. J. McGill & Impact Printing 2008.

Copyright of images belongs to the contributors and the original photographers:- Frank McCaughan, Sally Stelter, Patrick and Dr Anne Casement, John Nicholl, Gerrard McKinley, Tommy McDonald, Danny Morgan, David Speers, John Humphries, Jim Greer, William Boyd Wilson, Dervock Community Association and the Causeway Museum Service. The publisher has made every effort to acknowledge the copyright holders of the material in this book. We would like to hear from anyone whose rights have unwittingly been infringed.

I.S.B.N. 978-1-906689-09-4

All rights reserved. No part of this book may be reproduced in any form, by photocopying or by any electronic or mechanical means, including information storage or retrieval systems, without permission in writing from both the copyright owners and the publisher of this book.

Designed and printed by Impact Printing, Ballycastle.

Introduction

This idea of producing an album of Moyle Memories grew from the discovery of a collection of old family photographs belonging to my Grandmother. They included family members who had emigrated, as well as old photos of people and events around Ballycastle. Other photographs were loaned from family albums, photograph collections and the Causeway Museum Services archive. They have given me the opportunity to present you with an album of memories of people, places and events around the district of Moyle from 50 years ago and beyond.

I am grateful to everyone who contributed to the content of this book, especially my uncle Danny McGill for realising the value of the photographs, Frank McCaughan, Sally Stelter, Patrick and Dr Anne Casement, John Nicholl, Gerrard McKinley, Tommy McDonald, Danny Morgan, David Speers, John Humphries, Jim Greer, William Boyd Wilson, Dervock Community Association, Helen Perry of the Causeway Museum Service and last but by no means least, my mother and her old box camera.

I would also like to thank the McCaughan Group for sponsoring this project. Frank A. McCaughan first opened the doors of his pharmacy on Ann Street on February 2nd 1959 and this book is being sponsored as a way of celebrating Frank's 50 years of dispensing to the people and livestock in Moyle and beyond.

This book is a product of my interest in researching the history of our community and it will become a part of the Community Archive. I hope that it will encourage others to seek out and take greater care of old photographs and documents. They are often the only means of connecting us, where-ever we are in the world, with our shared past here in the District of Moyle.

Danny McGill.

Dedicated to emigrants everywhere!

Moyle Memories - 50 years and beyond.

Kate was a sister, a mother, an aunt and everyone's granny. She sat at the spinning wheel dreaming as she spun her wool, dreaming of friends and fairs from long ago. Boat trips and train rides. Long summer days and coming home with the hay. Friends and neighbours, working, playing and dancing. Grandchildren in their mother's arms, herself in hers. Loved ones now passed on, some to a better place, some to a better land. Her own childhood playmates sit by their firesides in distant places, in the suburbs and cities, prairie farms and forest cabins thinking of her and the good times they shared. In her pocket there's a letter telling her about the journey to a new home, the new job and a precious photo of her first grandchild. The letters are all creased and worn, the photo creased even more; precious memories, her treasure.

This album is intended to gather together some of those photos of people, places and events in Ballycastle and the surrounding villages. To try to tell their stories. These are the stories that belong to us all, some are our memories, some just beyond. So I've tried to draw them back so that we can all share them. They are our treasure, for us all to share.

This scene of Ballycastle in 1885 is a fine example of an image telling its own story. In the foreground is the railway cutting and to the right the little bridge. A telegraph pole stands on the bank with the thatched roof of Plumfall behind.

Beyond is the Fair Green. In the middle distance a group of school children are lined up, probably at the photographer's request, for what may be the earliest first school photo of Ballycastle children. To the left of centre is the Ballycastle Gas Works and beyond that Mill Street.

The new chapel on the hill replaces the old one here at the Fairhill. Charles Darragh a local stone mason built the Chapel spire, the O'Connor Memorial and carved the boy's head at the Pans Rocks, where the sandstone was quarried.

Staying in Glen Taisie, this group of pictures of Mill Street show us the homes of many of the craftsmen and workers who have lived on this site for generations.

The oldest one above, shows the mill on the right and some ancient cottages. The others were taken in the Fifties, not long before they fell to a road improvement scheme.

For a time the east end of Mill Street was home to Dusty Rhodes, and his third wife Rose Cameron. This is the Fifties with a Ford Prefect. The Milltown cottages pre-date most of the houses in Ballycastle which were built in the 1700's and later. Castle Street was mostly built in the C18th, but a number of small lanes of older cottages led off Castle Street, many surviving until the camera captured them forever. Their names include Nailor's Row, Union Row, Davy's Row, Boyd's Lane...

Castle Street was the dominant trading street in Ballycastle. This is where the merchants, who came to Ballycastle after Hugh Boyd built the harbour, set up in business. Many of them built their own premises. One shop surviving from those early days is Sharpe and McKinley.

The photograph shows the 'Count' McKinley entering his shop.

In living memory cattle filled the street on market days, from the Diamond to Mary McDonnell's Spirit Store on Castle Street.

This view of the top of Castle Street, shows a prosperous looking Mr Black outside his shop, and a number of bystanders along the street watching the photographer. Even the policeman has come out of the barracks for a look.

The rubbish in the street suggest that it was neither a Wednesday nor a Saturday, as these were the days when everyone was obliged, by a clause in their leases, to sweep the street in front of their premises and remove the rubbish.

As the main road into the town, Castle Street has seen a lot of unusual traffic. On the right the 'Count McKinley' is perusing some rare pedestrians on their way to the circus.

This is Rose McAlister, a straw hat maker, outside her shop in Castle Street. She was one of many crafts people working in the town at a time when only the wealthy could travel to buy their needs. Dressmakers and tailors were kept busy with local trade

This young lady is dressed in her best outside McAlister's hardware shop next door, at the corner of Clare Street and Castle Street. She's wearing a straw hat so maybe she's one of the family? Perhaps Mary Ann McAlister?

Even Clare Street above had its shops and workshops. At the north end was Nailor's Row - a noisy hive of industry. Clare Street was the home of the last Blacksmith's workshop in Ballycastle, run by Willie Parker.

On the left, looking up Castle Street, stands the Antrim Arms Hotel. The 'Classic Hotel and Restaurant' and Peter Dallat's shop, are on the right. The shop by the post box is Mooneys 'Boot & Shoe Warehouse'.

The poles mark the arrival of the telephone, each with its own wire. Further up the street there is a motor lorry, heralding the end of horse-drawn transport.

Soon some shops had their own liveried motor vans, though it was a good while before the horse finally gave way. Johnny Jennings' bread cart was one of the last horse-drawn traders' carts.

This aerial view of Castle Street is for you to explore for yourself. Look for the lanes of cottages and the Milltown. You can also see how wide Castle Street used to be, when the castle stood next to the Town Church, at the end of the Poor Row cottages.

After Hugh Boyd built the church in 1756 the area in front was called Church Square, but only after the river was closed over and the ground raised to form the Diamond. This became the centre of Ballycastle, with two new roads created to lead away from it - Market Street and the Tanyard Brae, often called Chapel Brae and now called Fairhill Street. Celebrations, markets and fairs have all assembled here, especially 'The Ould Lammas Fair'. How many of you remember the Steam Roundabout?

This view of the Diamond in 1929, shows how little the town has changed. The Royal, the Antrim Arms, Molloy's Diamond Bar & Restaurant (formerly McClements Spirit Store), McDonnell's and the Boyd Arms are all still with us, giving the Diamond a character all its own. The Fair Day (left) hasn't changed a bit, only the caps. The small group around a boy with a box still draws more in for that 'bargain', something to take back home to remind you of friends you met – until next year.

The fairs and Markets always drew a crowd and there was always another one somewhere: Armoy, Bushmills, or Dervock where the main street was just as crowded with men and animals. In Armoy the animals were tied up to rings set in the walls, the horses on Main Street and the cattle along Market Street.

This is the fair at its best. The stall at the front has 'sweety jars' to tempt the farthings from a child's hand. Another stall promises a glimpse of the future, others offer old clothes, china, glass and haberdashery. Note the mobile stall at the centre of the photo. If you got tired of the crowd you could retire to Hunter's Spirit Store or take a seat in the hairdressing saloon and chat to friends not met since last year.

Other fairs were held in season: Goose Fairs, Apple Fairs and Pig Fairs. There were also the Hiring Fairs in May and November, where workers were hopeful of finding a good employer for the next six months or a year. If they were lucky they would get a shilling or two in 'earnest' to spend at the fair.

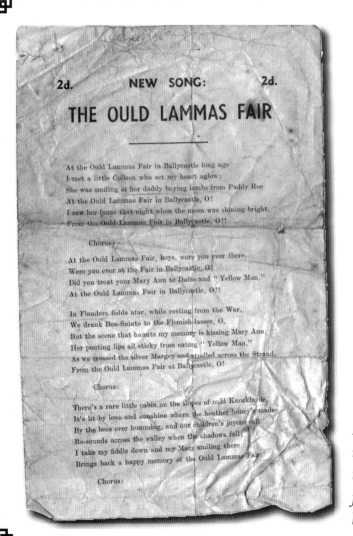

One of the many craftsmen in Ballycastle was John Henry MacAulay, who not only was a first class carver of bog oak, but was more famously the writer of 'The Ould Lammas Fair'. The lyrics tell the story of love, war and peace, from the Lammas Fair to Flander's fields and back to the slopes of Knocklayde, "where the heather honey's made".

A playful side to his character is revealed in a note ordering coal from John Nicholl.

Look at the list of items made from Bog Oak. The displays in the shop would have been very attractive with the black carvings mixed with the cream of the Belleek pottery. I see that he signs himself Carver.

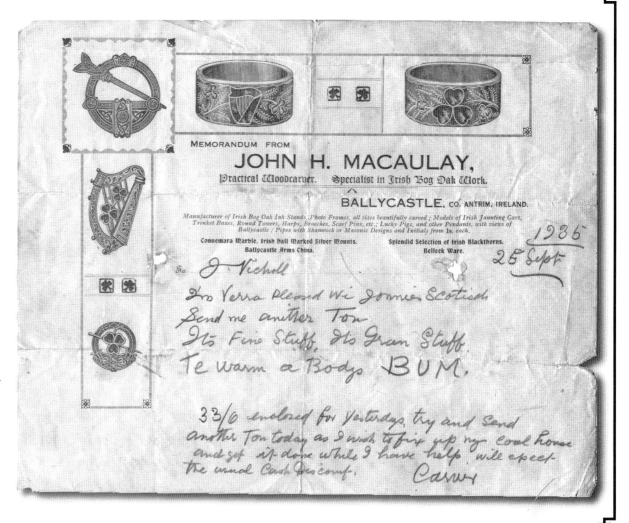

The lanes of Ballycastle and the Milltown were home to the workshops of Blacksmiths, Coopers and Carpenters. These trades were in demand, especially on market days when horses would be left in for new shoes, or a cart for a new shaft, or a set of iron tyres. Often the work would be done and payment promised for later in the season when the crops were in or stock sold. Many's the time a bill was chased around the pubs on market day and a drink was often more readily offered than the payment. One of these craftsmen had another skill, that of fiddle making.

John McGill was a coachbuilder who first set up in a workshop in the Milltown mill. His hobby was making fiddles. He made them out of wood, tin and even the perspex canopy of a crashed plane. Here he is at the fair.

Most of John's fiddles went to America. Many a tune was played on them down in his basement in Anne Street, which became known as 'Hell's Kitchen'. John had other skills too - growing tobacco was just one which guaranteed a well attended Ceilidh.

'Old John' famously turned down the offer of a Ford Agency, believing that the car would never replace the horse. In his later years he was known to advise people that 'opportunity only comes once in a lifetime'. When the coachbuilding and coopering gave out he turned his skills to house-building around Ballycastle and as far afield as Limavady.

At the top of North Street Yankee Dan Black built one of the finest boats ever to sail out of The Quay. Records show that the boat, Star of the Sea a 'One Mast Jib...Sail/Motor' was registered to his brother James. The dimensions of 35 feet by 10 feet 6 inches beam fits the description. Unfortunately she was lost within the year.

The photo shows her at the bottom of Rathlin Road. The story goes that it was safer to bring her down the Rathlin Road than straight down North Street. Dickie Duffin was one of the small boys in the photo. Some of them were going to fetch butter-milk, hence the cans. The photographer, Mr Coghlan of Castle Street, fortunately for us, spotted a great opportunity. It is very likely that the man in the tweeds is Yankee Dan himself, supervising the delivery.

Up to the early 1900s the fishermen rowed or sailed to the fishing banks near Rathlin Island. Then the power of the oarsmen and sails, was replaced with engines saved from scrapped cars. The fishermen from Donegal to the Glens, competed at the local Regattas. The sailing and rowing races were fiercely competitive. One famous boat, Port Moon's Arrow (safely stored locally by the National Trust) is still spoken of as being the fastest racing drontheim, on the Causeway Coast. This photograph of a Regatta in Ballycastle Bay around the 1890's, captures the closing stage of a rowing race, with the spectators crowding the rocks at Port Brittas.

The regattas brought crowds of people to see the races, in 1882 the railway company even put on 'specials' to come and see the Arrow race against Ballycastle boats like the Vulcan, Stag, and the Emily. Newspaper reports of the 1882 Ballycastle Regatta tell of a sunny breezy day which led to exciting sailing races. The result of the rowing event for 24 foot, four oared boats was 1st Arrow, 2nd Supple Kate (from Coleraine) and 3rd Vulcan.

In 1885 four of the Port Moon fishermen were drowned within sight of their home port. They were bringing a boat back from the Foyle, perhaps from Moville. A few years later the Arrow was crewed by Dunseverick fishermen. The Fishermen of Dunseverick by James McQuilken is an excellent account of their lives and times.

There was a 24 foot class for racing drontheims and 30 foot 4 oar boats. In 1876 Ballycastle's *Emily* was crewed by Jack Coyles, James Nicholl, Andy McLaughlin and A. Cook with A. Black as coxwain. In 1882 Ballycastle's *Vulcan* was crewed by D. Black, A. Black, J. Nicholl and J. Wilson.

This Rathlin Regatta race (above) looks like being a close finish. These are a larger class than the little boat on the right, which Jack Coyles is steering for the finishing line. Johnnie Coyles and Alex Morgan make up his crew.

I'm led to believe that the larger boat to the left is the Lively Lass of Ballycastle. Built in Portrush with a 22 foot keel. Here she is crewed by O'Connor, Jennings, Sammy Keane and Joe McCarthy. Perhaps someone can confirm that? Certainly this small collection gives us a good idea of what these Regattas were like all those years ago.

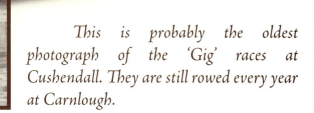

This is probably the oldest photograph of the 'Gig' races at Cushendall. They are still rowed every year at Carnlough.

These are the Regatta Accounts from 1891. This is only the first page of the list of contributions from Ballycastle residents. The biggest contribution was from the Member of Parliament Sir Charles Lewis.

Interestingly the 'Ass Race' cost 17/6d and the band cost more than the Boat Races. I see they valued advertising as they paid for adverts in seven newspapers. It's no surprise that the Regatta was well attended.

These scenes of Ballycastle Regatta from the 1930's, will never be seen again. The boats were mainly working boats of a type long passed out of daily use. The successful Ballintoy crew stand in front of their boat after winning the race for 20 footers.

These boatmen were the last of their ilk. Men whose lives depended on working with nature in the raw. Their ports were stony beaches or gaps in the rocks all along the coast. These romantic images are all they leave behind of their recreation, their boats and their little ports, like this one at Kenbann. They belie the harsh reality of their daily lives.

The regatta races were the lighter side of life along the north coast. The treacherous sea, where these men spent their working lives, was a harsh workplace. The Nordic clinker-built double ended drontheim boats suited the sea conditions.

Jack Coyles, who for years carried the Rathlin mails, spent his life like many others, maintaining links with Rathlin in all weathers. He once said that with a double ended clinker boat, you got a lift from a following sea and as many keels as there were planks in the water. He loved his little home port at the 'Quay', the boat slip at Port Brittas, because 'whatever the sea', he told me, 'you could run up the beach, step out and go for your tea'.

Other boatmen along the coast were not so lucky as Jack. Fishermen from Port Moon, Dunseverick and Ballintoy were often caught out near the 'Bull' with a load of fish and a storm coming in from the north-west. They had a hard row home against the elements.

Ballycastle Bay was claiming boats as long as there were men to sail them. Hugh Boyd lost four while building the harbour, the Maidenhead full of timber was his last. The sailing ships were at the mercy of the tides and storms, especially if the sailors were strangers.

In modern times the steam powered ships were no more fortunate. Here are two ships aground at the foot of Fair Head. The Garnes and the Glentow, the one saved and the other lost.

In 1917 an incoming convoy of ships from America was attacked by the German submarine U79. The Royal Navy cruiser H.M.S. Drake was the first to be torpedoed and drifted out of control between Fair Head and the Rue Point at the southern tip of Rathlin. The Mendip Range, (left) on an easterly course through Rathlin Sound, tried unsuccessfully to avoid the collision, after which the master ran her aground on Ballycastle Strand. The vessel was later re-floated and eventually reached Glasgow for repairs. Before it was floated off the strand, hundreds of bags of flour were auctioned off, possibly to lighten the ship.

H.M.S. Brisk *(on the right), a destroyer escorting the same convoy, was also sunk, along with the cargo vessel* Lugano, *which was carrying cotton, alcohol and steel. They both lie on the seabed near Carrickmannon rock.*

Two other unusual visitors arrived in the bay during the Forties or Fifties; Norwegian Whaling Catchers. These small vessels would chase whales and harpoon them, after which they would take them to the much larger factory ship for processing. For many years whaling activities provided valuable lamp oil, meat and fats to produce margarine. The traditional shape of the whalers is similar to Norwegian fishing boats of today. The sea around the north coast is not known for great numbers of whales, so why were these boats here?

Another surprise for Ballycastle people was about 1937 when the airship *Hindenburg* flew over. It was seen coming in and heading up the glen. At least three people told me about it: my grandfather, John McGill, Jimmy McNeill and Kathleen McCann, whose father rushed in and carried her up the cliff to see it floating up the glen. Another unexpected visitor to the bay was an R.A.F. glider, which made an emergency landing on the strand.

These two photos have the look of organised events, though none the less interesting. The rescue helicopter is a Sycamore and the other an earlier Sikorsky, both military aircraft.

In 1931 a seaplane arrived in the bay, on the day Ramsey MacDonald came to visit Rathlin Island. An account of the day said that the sea was like glass, the best day all year.

The plane was a Supermarine Southampton, based at Oban. With it's eight man crew, it was the most advanced military combat plane of its day.

The local boatmen spent the day taking the townsfolk out to see it.

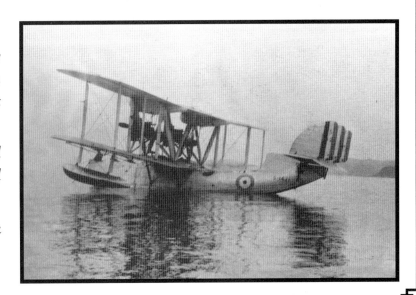

This view of the 'Quay' has a great deal to tell us. From right to left we have the 'boat slip' with the Blacksmith's forge at the top and the new houses on North Street behind. The white buildings are the Coast Guard Station, with their flag flying. The Kelp Store, in the middle, is probably the oldest building in the Ballycastle area. In front of this is the fishermen's net drying green, with a few boats drawn up.

The rocks on the foreshore are the remnants of Hugh Boyd's harbour wall. The wall on the left edge of the photo is around Humphreys' Coalstore, the site of the first wireless station in Ireland. It was established by the Marconi Company for Lloyds to communicate shipping news from Rathlin Island. The port is named after a Viking, **Brittas**, though map makers in the 18th century changed it to *British Port* for a while.

Hugh McGildowney built a pier at the Scarf rock. His little puffer Glentow was one of the boats which revitalised Ballycastle's economy, exporting limestone from the Whiterocks, to the iron smelting furnaces in Scotland and returning with Scottish coal from Kilmarnock. The steam crane did much of the lifting and a tramway ran the full length.

Hugh McGildowney planned an extension of the little narrow gauge railway from the town to the collieries and back along the shore to the Quay, but it never came to be.

Any boat moored at the pier was exposed to the swell, but with the trammers and the steam crane, loading and unloading was necessarily fairly quick.

Some rare treasures came to light recently, showing piers being built, repaired or being cut up. This very early photo from about the year 1900, shows building work at the old boat slip or 'Port Brittas'. Note the men working with the old style crane. In fact it looks as though it was taken when an inspection 'committee' were visiting the work. There are two bowler hats and two watch chains on view. The third man seems to be pointing out something to the first two. In the foreground a boat appears to be loading up for Rathlin. At the end of the pier a second crane with a longer boom, is unloading stone from a boat. Note the shuttering and 'B Castle' on the sailing boat.

The Glentow *steaming back to Ballycastle for another load of limestone.*

The Glentow *along with the* Drake *is our best known wreck. She was lost aground at Fair Head in 1915. Here she is at McGildowney's pier being unloaded by one of the steam cranes.*

These scrap iron men are cutting up the old McGildowney's pier. The pier had a short life and was dependant on trade with McGildowney's own puffers. With the Glentow and himself gone it fell into disuse.

By 1931 the Urban District Council had decided to build a new pier between Port Brittas and McGildowney's pier. The work was well in hand by 1934.

The new pier is shown here still under construction. Sections were shuttered and the concrete poured, so it looked like it was built with concrete Lego. This is still evident in the remaining section of the pier.

These workmen are left to right: William Colgan, Jimmy McGowan, John Cranen, William Dunlop and John McBride. The photo was taken by John McAfee.

Still at the Quay this photo shows the first ship to unload coal at the new pier, the Ben Maye. Note the men hauling the chaldrons of coal, loading them on to Nicholl's lorry. In the boat slip luggage and passengers are being loaded for Rathlin Island.

Compare this scene with the earlier photo of the boat slip workers.

An indication of the problems that the new pier would face can be seen here, where the gentle swell of the sea comes round the end of the pier.

One of the first ships to experience the swell at the new harbour was the Ben Maye *(top left). Her mooring ropes held, but unfortunately the* Serb's *broke, though thankfully she was not lost, just a few bruised plates and some unwanted ballast. The new 1934 pier was the scene of a few near disasters. It was fine in a calm sea but any sort of a swell would overtop the pier wall giving many people a soaking. The swell was strong enough to break a mooring line resulting in another job for the salvage men.*

This pier was a good fishing spot. You could watch the fish swimming around your bait, so even if you didn't catch anything you could at least see why.

On fine summer afternoons many budding Cross-Channel swimmers used to swim from the pier to the little strand. In the evenings shoals of Mullet would tantalise the best of fishermen, who could do nothing but watch the fishs' graceful parade along the harbour wall.

A busy day at the new pier was Rathlin Sports Day, which brought a number of boats to the quay, loading people for the island.

CE54 (below) was Robert McMullan's 27 foot motorboat Rowan *from Dunseverick, taking people over for the sports. The smaller CE54 at the pier above was a later boat from the Fifties- that looks like the* Star of the Sea *at the end of the pier.*

Rathlin Sports Day was a popular event. Teams from Armoy and Ballycastle used to compete with the Rathlin men in the Tug-of-War.

Competitors in the 1-mile running races included James McMullan, Frank McCurdy and Paddy McQuilken.

In 1937 Jack Coyles's father had two new motor boats built by Kellys of Portrush. Jack was sent to help work on them. When the day came to bring them home, Jack's father started to launch one, when old Mr Kelly stopped him and said, 'you canny launch her without a name'. So Jack's father said 'well we better name her after him that's getting crowned today then'. So old Mr Kelly reached into his pocket for chalk and the name King George VI was written on her bow and away they went. It was Coronation Day in 1937. Jack worked the Rathlin mails and passenger trade with the King George VI until poor health made him retire, just after he'd done up her engine too! Here's the boat getting ready to accompany Jack McClelland on his swim from Rathlin to Ballycastle. The man filling her up is Jim Curry.

This photo was taken before the first war, about 1906. The boatmen are getting ready to take a shooting party to Rathlin.

Quite often a pleasant morning 'going for a sail' turned into a stormy sea by afternoon and many day trippers to Rathlin either ended up being tossed about under Fair Head on a stormy trip home, or finding a spot to sleep on the floor of McQuig's pub.

These photos taken in 1903 show the wreck of the trawler Starling keeled over in the harbour. She hit Carrickmannon Rock, off Kenbann Head. The salvage boat George Lindsey is waiting to recover her.

Perhaps a portable canvas boat on the garden pond at Magherintemple was a safer place than Rathlin Sound. No Atlantic swell or tide-rips to worry about and not far to shore when its time for tea.

Before we leave Port Brittas and memories of sunny afternoons playing safely in the sea, there are one or two old photos which will help explain the changes that have gone on here over the years. Looking back towards the Marine corner, the ruins of Boyd's west pier wall can be seen. Where Hugh Boyd had created a 'dockside' area, the sea has breached the wall and removed the 'fill' creating a new beach and 'slip' for the safe storage of the fishing boats. This area has been reclaimed again and is now used as a car park. Note the old harbour wall in front of the Marine. This bank of rocks on the right, are all that remains of Hugh Boyd's east pier, which even though the harbour was filled with sand, still protected the boat slip when the Margy was in flood. Now it is part of the Marina defences.

Here we see the funfair in the pier yard in the Forties. The postcard shows the Coastguard Station painted white, with the forge at the top of the boat slip.

The curved top of Humphreys' coalstore tells us that it has, by this time, been converted into a garage to store the motorcars of the more well-off Quay residents.

The wall of Humphreys' yard is on the left next to the side-car, in this view of Little North Street or Bayview Road.

Visitors to Ballycastle always enjoyed a stroll along 'Glass Island' where a footbridge was built across the Margy giving them access to the beach and the new bathing huts.

Here's a happy family enjoying the sunshine on the strand.

The photo was taken not long before they emigrated to England in 1951.

These Rathlin visitors around 1900 have plenty of baggage for their holiday on the island. This group below included one Fergus Grieve, who in 1901, was on the island and went collecting bird's eggs with Paddy the 'Cliff Climber'. Equipped with a stout rope, the islanders would collect seabirds' eggs from the cliffs. Note the Puffin on the ropes, they were so tame that they were caught for food in the past.

The lady in this photo is Rose McCurdy, Fergus is second from the left. Note the thatch on the cottage. The islanders relied on fishing and a little farming.

Does anyone know these Rathlin men have been out shooting wildfowl? The port may possibly be O'Byrne. Unfortunately I can find no name or number on the boats. The date would be around 1900.

This young man looks ready for the yacht races. Who was he, a visitor? Perhaps he's not on Rathlin, but Ballintoy or Dunseverick? The dried fish may be a clue.

Stock raised on the island had to be taken by boat to Ballycastle for market. This involved 'hog tying' the animals for the journey, laid on a bed of hay in the bottom of the boat.

In this later photograph the men and the boats have changed, but the method of handling the beasts is just the same.

Here's another passenger for the boat back to Ballycastle. This time it's the policeman who has been over taking the census.

Occasionally a new family member was brought home to see Granny. This family group photo is dated around 1925 and the family are believed to be McQuilkens.

All too soon they had to return to the mainland.

This pier was built at Killeaney in 1922. For a short time there was work quarrying limestone. Here the trucks have been filled ready for the next boat to take it to Scotland. The islanders have always been able to turn their hands to anything. This lady has a fine ladder for her work repairing the thatch.

Photos of daily work are few, unless the workers are doing something unusual, such as building a railway or a pier. Fishermen and farmers were always more interesting to the first photographers, who wanted romantic images to sell to the city folk.

We are fortunate in having a few personal photos from the early years of the 20th century. Nicholl's Brickyard and Sawmill in Glentow was very active in providing building material for the growing town. Hand-made bricks were laid out to dry in rows and covered with straw, before firing in the kiln.

Here we have not only the brickyard and the railway, you can also see the old road from Glenshesk as it turns the corner to come down to the river. Then the road crossed over the bridge to the bottom of Bleachgreen Avenue.

Along the river Tow, on the other side of the railway viaduct, was the saw mill, which was originally water powered. Logs wait to be sorted and sawn. Beyond a stack of sawn timber, motor and horsedrawn transport stand in front of the storage racks.

When the railway came they laid a small branch line down to the yard. This brought the timber in directly from the docks to the mill. The trucks were let down the slope by a windlass and turned into the mill yard on a turntable, which can be seen above. The boys on the right are the brick making crew.

Before we go much further let me introduce you to some of the workers. Here are some of Ballycastle's finest, the predecessors of the volunteer firemen of today, with their Green Goddess fire-engine.

This group of ladies were doing their best to help the war effort by collecting paper salvage.

Although not voluntary, these two men performed a useful task for Ballycastle people. Mr Elliott and his son photographed in the 1950's, standing next to the old Ballycastle Urban Council, Cleansing Department's dustcart.

Another group of volunteers vital for any maritime community, are the fishermen and boatmen themselves. On numerous occasions they have risked their own lives to rescue seamen from stricken wrecks. There were two notable occasions when the Rathlin Life Saving Company risked their lives. One dark, stormy night they were called out to rescue the crew of the trawler *Shackleton* which struck the rocks on the north side of the island. Years later they also rescued the crew of the *Pintail*.

The fascinating stories of Rathlin's wrecks and rescues are illustrated and detailed in three books: *Augustine McCurdy's* Rathlin's Rugged Story, *Alex Morrison's*, Rathlin Island As I Knew It, *and Tommy Cecil's* , The Harsh Winds of Rathlin.

Here the Island men are receiving their well earned testimonials in recognition of the Shackleton rescue. The only one I can name is Jim McCurdy on the far right.

Many years later their bravery was acknowledged again with the second award of the National Life Saving Shield for saving the crew of the Pintail.

These next photos do show some workers, though you'll have to search for them. There are some above ground, but most of them are down in the depths digging coal.

This is the pithead at Ballyreagh mine. Notice the men on the top of the winding gantry. Coal was worked in this area for hundreds of years ending in the 1950's. Along the shore the coal mines were originally worked to feed the salt pans, then exports to Dublin in the 1750's. Later the iron ore mines were worked at Carrickmore, where the ore was calcined by burning with local coal and the resulting product sent to Scotland.

The Belfast Coal and Iron Company found a seam of clay at the mine which they used to produce chimney pots, garden pots and bricks. The resulting pottery was a pale yellow colour. There are still a few Ballyreagh Chimney pots on local houses.

This photo shows the brickworks in the background. The chimney was quite a landmark, but all that remains now is a bumpy field.

These were sent from Glasgow to my Grandmother. They record the boys growing up, perhaps her nephews.

The same boys are shown a few years older, then two more photos show them as young men in uniform, one in the merchant navy the other in the army.

This set of portraits is an excellent example of families keeping in touch through photographs.

The donkey cart was the reliable transport for many people, carrying their goods wherever they were needed. The donkey cart could get into places a motor could not and its large wheels could roll over the roughest ground. It could be safely driven by small boys, who doubtless enjoyed the freedom it gave them and I'm sure the donkey knew where he was going anyway.

All he needed was a bit of hay and a warm bed with the occasional rub of the head just to let him know you hadn't forgotten him.

The slipe car was so simple it could get through rough ground to places wheels couldn't.

A faster means of personal transport was the Pony and Trap. Many families had their own, especially the farming community. The Pony, like the Donkey knew his way home, he didn't need any 'sat-nav'. Citybound Victorian tourists loved the freedom of the little Trap as they roamed the beautiful Glens of Antrim.

How many of you know where the hotel was?

The sturdy farm cart was often called into passenger service, especially to entertain visitors 'back home' for the holidays.

This party with John and Ann Casement at Magherintemple in the early 1900s, are setting off round the farm for a picnic. The horse may well have enjoyed a change of scenery too and probably an odd apple from the picnic basket.

Agriculture is a great part of our heritage and the farmer's pride in his animals and his work has given us many good photos like this fine young bull, at Casement's.

Ploughing matches are where some of that pride is demonstrated. A well presented pair of horse and a straight furrow won the day then just as they do today.

The ploughman on the right, had already spent hours grooming and dressing his horses, before winning another prize for his employer, walking alongside.

Later in the year there are oats to be harvested and potatoes to be gathered from this field near the town.

After the harvest there's ploughing to be done before the Lammas floods arrive.

This field on Rathlin must be fairly light as Owen Murphy is able to plough it with one horse. There appears to be a field of potato rigs or 'lazy beds' on the hillside beyond.

Mickey Doran from Dervock is harrowing, making a fine tilth, photographed here with his dog and two horses, though one seems to be attempting a conversation with the photographer.

No collection of agricultural memories would be complete without the little tractor. This one even has blinkers on, a requirement during the war to prevent lights showing skywards. What was it doing in the lanes - delivering peats, or collecting boys for a day's work on the farm? The shadows show early afternoon. This is thought to be New Row off Castle Street.

Below we have Jack Coyles on the left with Pete Tomilty (?), Johnny McQuilken, Bertie Coyles, Tony McCuaig and Bill Curry with a brand new tractor outside McQuig's pub on Rathlin Island.

A calf sale in Carey was often hard work for the auctioneer, Pat McCambridge. Here he seems to be working hard to get a decent bid.

Here's another 'wee fergy' bringing home the hay at Ffiarne. The badge on the grill tells us it is fitted with a Perkins diesel engine. P.J. Gillan is driving with his father Joe behind. Mikey and Tony on the top of the load are ready for their tea. Putting the hay in the loft was a lot easier with the bales, not as dusty a job as packing it in loose and it didn't itch so much either!

Threshing with steam engines was usually done by contractors moving from farm to farm. Here on a Glens farm they have started soon after the harvest.

Raising Turkeys was a profitable enterprise, often reserved for the farmer's wife. This fine flock with their tails up at Magherintemple look ready for the Christmas market.

A good many pigs faced the same fate as the Turkeys. This young sow has just landed at the boatslip from Rathlin Island. Her companion is being off-loaded.

This last view brings us back to Ballycastle, to the Hillhead farm of Jim Greer J.P., with a lively flock of lambs. The solitary house is on Ramoan Road is now surrounded by dwellings.

When Hugh Boyd died he left money for retired workers' cottages to be build near the church. The 'Poor Row', as it became known, was a lane of cottages all with half doors and a good-sized south-facing garden. There was even a plot of ground on Market Street set aside, where they could keep their manure.

Angus Patton was one resident who is remembered as living both here and in New Row off Castle Street.

Memories of the sun shining through the half-doors into the little cottages still lingers with many Ballycastle folk.

This is the beginning of the end for Poor Row.

This aspect of the railway embankment and station gives us a different view of the Poor Row cottages, with their south-facing gardens.

North Street around 1900. Strandview Road is not yet constructed and the little thatched cottages in the way look to be derelict. Three buildings in this photo are still standing: Brian Boyle's old shop, Humphrey's Post Office, and my first home at 18 North Street. The tree on the corner, by the pump, still shelters us from summer showers.

Left is a closer view of the last few thatched cottages at the Quay. Rosemary Cottage (above) was the one further up the street. You can see from this photograph that the lower cottage was extended to two stories not long after. Here the roof is being slated.

This photo shows Chapel Lane, more familiarly known today as Fairhill Street or Tanyard Brae. The entry to the Milltown is on the right. That looks like a cart with no wheels against the ditch. The roof in the top right looks like a Belfast Truss roof. The roof beams, or trusses were made up of a lattice of light battens, with the trademark curved roof which was boarded, then covered in felt or canvas and tar, making a very light roof. This enabled wider spacing in a building for workshops, stores etc. Tilly Molloy's in Armoy had such a roof, providing an open space for a hall below.

Quay Road was a popular promenade as can be seen here in this 1900 view looking up the road from the corner of the new Marine Hotel, built on the site of the old Customs House and the first Inn at the Quay. The Manor House on the left was still home to the Boyd family. Note the portico, the railings, the gaslamp and a bollard to prevent carts cutting the corner.

The area opposite the Manor House was originally the carriage turn for the house. Later it was chosen for the site of the War Memorial. This rare photo of Miss Boyd with the ex-servicemen was taken on a Remembrance Sunday in the 1930's.

The Victorian houses which give Quay Road its unique character, were mostly built around 1900. This sylvan scene shows a workman at the present entrance to Mowbray House. The Avenue was planted by Hugh Boyd about 1750.

The great Blizzard of 1947 brought a fall of snow which lay around in the hollows of Knocklayde until June. Jimmy McNeill remembers making snowshoes out of boards so they could walk on it where it was deep. At one place in Carey the snow had drifted so deep that the telegraph poles became mere stumps sticking out of the ground. North Street and the Quay Road became playgrounds for snowballing, slides and toboganning.

A hardy lad could fly down North Street and end up round the Marine Corner if he was brave enough to hang on. Some didn't have such fast sleighs, so an old bath had to do them. This photo shows Mary and Johnny McGill with Patrick Collins in the bath, in North Street. The bigger lads took to the frozen Margy where they played ice hockey, Ballycastle style.

This probably is the most famous photo of the Ballycastle Railway. Danny McGill of Ann Street, took this shot and a few others of the train snowed in at Balleeny. The train had already ploughed through a few small drifts, but when it got to the start of the embankment the snow had drifted too much for it to push through.

A few boys got a ride out from Ballycastle on a waggon with the men who dug out the little Number 41. Once the line was clear it proved itself as a lifeline during the Big Snow. The children going to school on the train from Armoy had a great time reaching out of the windows to grab snow for snowball fights. This looks like another mishap in the snow, with number 44 needing a lift with the crane.

Here we have Barry Limerick, the engine driver, on the footplate with Jack McDuff, the fireman. He's got her steamed up and ready for the long haul up the gradient to Capecastle. This is Jack's own fireman's manual which explains how to burn the coal in the grate in such a way that the temperature in the boiler stays constant.

The little narrow gauge railway gave holiday makers, farmers and locals more than 50 years' service. The frequent stops along the way meant that it was used as a local service and gave the country people access to the mainline connection at Ballymoney.

Ballycastle even had a stock yard for the waggon loads of cattle waiting for market. The Lammas Fair meant 'specials' carrying visitors. One, in 1898, was Guilgemo Marconi who visited his wireless stations here and on Rathlin.

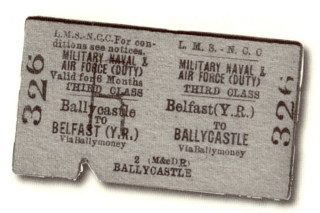

The Narrow Gauge Railway really opened up opportunities for Ballycastle workers. They were able to buy a 'workman's' season ticket and go off to work in the surrounding area on the early morning 'workman's special'. This special ticket was issued to services personnel.

As well as providing a passenger service, transport for heavy materials and livestock, the railway also carried mail and parcels. However it was all replaced in July 1950 by the new buses, which I suppose did at least go places even the little narrow gauge couldn't.

When the last train left Ballycastle in July 1950, it was covered in Christmas tinsel, leaving behind a few carriages in the sidings to be used as holiday caravans.

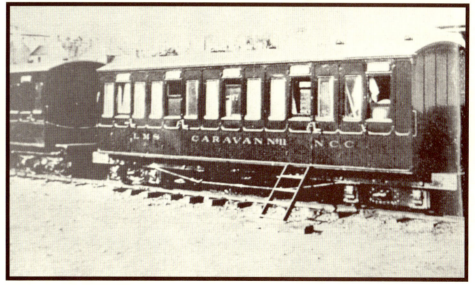

The villages around Ballycastle provide us with a variety of interesting photographs. This early photo of the Carrick-a-Rede Rope Bridge shows the precarious nature of the bridge when going across really was a challenge, especially with an armful of fishing gear, or riding a bike!

Nearby Ballintoy Harbour exported limestone and the thousands of cobble stones for the streets of Britain and America.

This is Ballintoy village on a quiet day. I wonder what the Victorian visitors thought of the little thatched Ballintoy Hotel here on the left with the porch.

This view from the east end of the village shows more thatched cottages and a barracks. Straw hats seem to have been popular with young ladies of the day. The tilting light in the window of the house on the right is a novel feature.

At the west end of Whitepark Bay, Port Braddon occupies a small area between the cliffs and the sea. As you can see the little port was just a rocky shore. The boat by the house looks to be a drontheim called the Sheila.

Below is Dunseverick Harbour, with Portmoon under the cliffs in the distance.

This old postcard shows the fishing nets drying at the home of the Arrow.

The tiny village nearby hasn't changed in years.

Samuel Johnson said the Giant's Causeway was "worth seeing, but not worth travelling to see". Thousands of visitors have disagreed with him and the Causeway is now a World Heritage Site. Who had the house by the shore is a mystery.

At Bushmills the Distillery has drawn equally large numbers of visitors and has been the economic support for a great many families over the years.

The river Bush has provided a pastime for locals and visitors, the one watching the other attempting to catch the king of fish. No pressure there then with the gallery above, the river too low and a hot mid-day sun.

The Bridge End Bar and the Refreshments Rooms await the tales of the disappointed fisherman and the millwheel waits for the ripening grain.

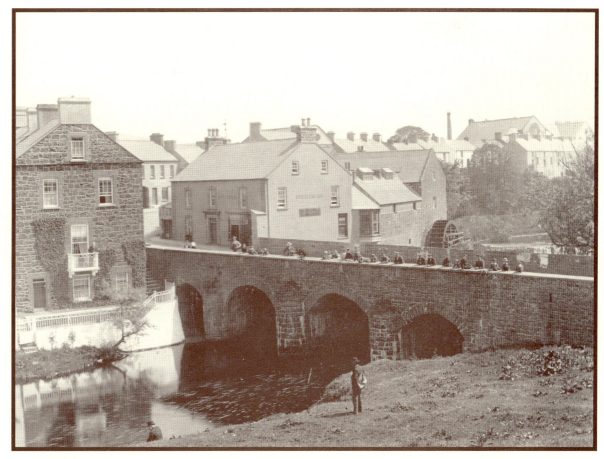

Main St. Dervock, Co. Antrim.

Further inland Dervock seems just as quiet as Armoy. Tilly Molloys to the right of the tree was the social centre for a great many people from the glen and the village. The Molloy family put on film shows, dances and had a little sweet shop. At one time they even bottled their own ginger beer.

THE FOUNTAIN, DERVOCK.

New Bridge View, Armoy

Another hopeful fisherman with an audience, this time on the River Bush at Armoy.

One of Ballycastle's many general stores was McCambridge's, on the corner of Market Street and Ann Street.

Armoy had Wilson's - that's him in the bowler hat. Dervock had Patrick's and Lochead or Thompson's shop. Who are the ladies?

These images bring back memories of blue sugar bags, food coupons and collecting Cod Liver Oil from the Dalriada Dance Hall.

Very little remains the same here on Ann Street. The trees on the left have all been replaced by shops and houses. The buildings on the right are recognisable, but those at the top of the street have been rebuilt. Behind the wall on the left is the lane of workshops and cottages called Harriet's or Billy's Lane, while the big house on the right was the Manse.

Before Anne Street was built in the 1750s, the town was connected to the Quay by a narrow lane behind the houses on the right.

    I'd be surprised if anyone remembers these two shops on the right. Joseph Moore appears to be a dealer in travel trunks and cases, an indication perhaps of the new mobility and emigration. All the shops beyond are newly built, reflecting a new age of prosperity. D. McHenry's shop appears to be selling china ornaments and glassware. If anyone has a pair of old Staffordshire dogs, that may be them in the window.

    These premises are now home to the Post Office and McCaughan's Chemists, where, before you could buy objects to decorate your home, perfumes and make-up now fill the shelves waiting to enhance the features of Ballycastle's young ladies, of all ages. Note the smocks and straw hats of the two girls walking past the old Manse. A good number of the trees Hugh Boyd planted to enhance his Anne Street from here to the quay can be seen here.

1937 saw the Coronation of King George VI and a parade through Ballycastle with speeches on the Diamond. Ballycastle folk like a parade and any chance to dress up.

Here are two characters who could always be found in any fancy dress parade - Jim McGill and 'Big Andy' McKinley, both dressed as washer women. The wee girl in pig tails next to them is Peter Molloy and the accordianist is Geordie McKay. The lorry belonged to Gallagher's Dairy.

Where are they now, Robin Hood, the Board Resident, the Minstrels, the Black Cat, the Flapper and the visitors from Mars?

We've met a few characters. Here are some that couldn't be left out. Who are these happy barefoot pupils? Look at little Mr Grumpy seated on the right in the second row. Who could resist such a happy band?

These children are hard at work at school on Rathlin.

In 1934 the modern world came to Ballycastle. The CINEMA opened in Market Street and for threepence you could spend the afternoon in Chicago as Al Capone or Tom Mix being chased through the canyons by Red Indians on the plains of the Wild West.

Ballycastle was no stranger to the theatre, the Dalriada Players regularly performed in the McAlister Hall, with musical interludes.

The motorcycle and side car was a popular means of transport. Just inside the garage is a wicker sidecar attached to a mystery motorbike, registration IA 677(?). Is this the first petrol station in Ballycastle?

This Douglas from the twenties was the star of its day, though the sidecar would have slowed it down. The Douglas was a great favourite for racing and trials.

The 1930 Ariel 500 was the road machine in its day too. Motorbikes were fairly cheap to run and owning a bike meant freedom to travel where you wanted for work or for pleasure.

Personal transport relied for years on a good horse or a pony and trap. You could always pedal of course, like these two who were so proud of their bikes that they had their photos taken with them.

This is Harry outside Hybla in 1913.

If you lived just out of Ballycastle the ride in was downhill and fast. The road home was harder, but at least the bike would carry your goods as you walked home.

We don't know who this gentleman is, the local Doctor perhaps?
This is a fast, sturdy rig with a strong pony in the shafts, perfect for the Glen roads.

With the advent of personal motor transport came the inevitable traffic accident. This one, on a sunny day in Mary Street, is very interesting. First there are two cars involved. The car nearest the camera sports an AA badge, while the car which struck it is a good way down the road in the side of a bus, with the usual group of onlookers. There are about ten buses parked along the roadside. Was it a Fair Day? Fortunately Ballycastle had it's own hospital in the old workhouse building and a fine new Ambulance which was substantially funded by Mrs King of Silversprings. Here she is standing next to Dr Boylan at the old hospital.

This van, parked at the bottom of Drumavoley, dates from the late Forties. Yes it does say Gartconney. Perhaps someone can tell us more?

Moving over the mountain for a look at some old photos of the Glens, these fine motors at Delargy's Hotel would fetch a good price today. That's a weighing machine behind the three gentlemen, very popular in a time of 'Health and Beauty'. The registration of the two seater 'tourer' with the 'Dickey seat' is XI 6445.

More old cars and another motor shop just next to the two cars. A 'Shell' sign indicates that they sold cans of petrol. This is another street scene that has changed very little, though I think the Temperance Hotel has closed. This later photo of the Red Arch shows that the road surfaces have by now been 'tarmacadamed', putting the old roadmen out of a job. They had the responsibility for filling in any 'potholes' along their stretch of the road. The hard iron wheels of the carts rutted them in the winter. When the pneumatic tyre came along it created a suction as it passed, lifting stones and dust, creating even more holes than before.

This is McNaughten, the roadman at Glenravel in 1910, talking to Mr Casement, with Terry the dog.

These two idyllic scenes of Cushendun don't tell the story of the harsh existence of many people living in these isolated rural communities.

The old mill on the quay had by this time been converted into McBride's Hotel.

Since the early 1900's Ballycastle has hosted an annual Tennis tournament on the new tennis courts on Hugh Boyd's inner dock. The dock had been used in the 1800's as the town dump, after which it was grassed over for the bowling green, then the tennis courts. Across the Margy the Golf Club boasted a nine hole course, expanding to a full course of 18 holes by 1912.

These golfers from February 1912 are Mr Casement, Miss Douglas, Daisy Weatherall, Mr B. Casement and Mr Davis. The photograph was taken in 1912 on the veranda of the new clubhouse.

This group of ladies are (from left to right): Sophy Hutchinson, Mary Bernard, Miss Kathleen Boyd holding the golf bag, Miss Miller in a white jacket, Daisy Weatherall behind, S. Blacker seated, Miss Douglas in the black hat, L. Barns and Harriet with the dog. Behind her is Miss Moorhead, with J Boyd, Miss Jackson and Miss Kirkpatrick at the back and last but not least H. Boyd and Miss Jackson at the front. The photo was taken in March 1912.

For many years part of the golf course was laid out as a sports arena and used every year for Ballycastle Sports day. The warren was a great place for the track as any rain soon drained away.

The crowds show that the cycle racing was very popular at the Sports day. This must have been like a fair day. Can you see one cyclist in the bottom right corner and another across the other side of the track?

At Cushendall Sports the same competitions where just as fiercely pursued, whether running or cycling. Here C. Black is winning the running race and W. McCormick of Ballycastle is pedalling for victory in the cycle race.

Remember the Ass Race in the 1891 Regatta Accounts? Their popularity survived longer than all the other events, they were still very popular when the sports transferred to Grottery Park.

This is the best Sports Day photo ever, where's donkey number two? Is that a wee McAleese galloping away in the middle? He looks as though he's ridden before.

Going back to the shore, the Pans Rocks were the location for the swimming club started by Mr Rooney in 1931. They managed to raise funds for diving boards and an annual swimming gala which was always well attended.

BALLYCASTLE AQUATICS.

COMPETITIONS AT PANS ROCK.

A varied programme of aquatic sports was staged at the Pans Rock bathing-place, Ballycastle, on Thursday afternoon, in aid of the fund for improving the bathing-place. The sports were organised by Mr. M. J. Rooney, who secured valuable assistance from Mr. and Mrs. Brown, Ardaghmore, Ballycastle, and members of the C.S.S.M. There was a large gallery of spectators, and the sports proved most successful. Mr. Wigram acted as starter, and the judges were Captain A. W. Cowdy and Mr. Martin Harvey.

The competitions were reported in the local press. Prizes were awarded for events which included: Boys' and Girls' relay races, the Biggest Splash competition, an Umbrella race, Diving, Dead Man's Floating race, a competition for the most original way of entering the water, a Balloon race, a Comic Dress competition and Pillow Fight. Diving exhibitions were also given at intervals during the afternoon.

Migration is part of our culture. We are all descended from waves of immigrants from Europe and beyond; for the simple reason that ten thousand years ago our part of this island was buried under a mile of ice. Bands of stone-age people came here and some went on elsewhere. The Vikings and the Normans followed and history records their story. In this modern age of writing and photography ordinary people are able to tell their stories of new worlds and send a photo home to the family to show how well they were doing. This photo shows the Jefferson family, who emigrated from the Bushmills area to somewhere near Stag Island, close to the Canadian border with the U.S.A. Take a close look at everything that is on display and you will see what I mean when I say, you can read the story in a picture and don't have to be able to write it down. Imagine a son or a daughter with their new spouse emigrating and their families never expecting to see them again. Then a photograph turns up in the post and there they are standing outside their new home and there's the children too...The photo answers all the questions for the anxious parents and the neighbours.

Daniel McKinley of Sharpe & McKinley, of Castle Street, was an agent for the White Star Line. Some passengers paid their own way while others travelled as 'Emigrants' at special rates who then travelled 'Steerage' which, as they say, is altogether another story.

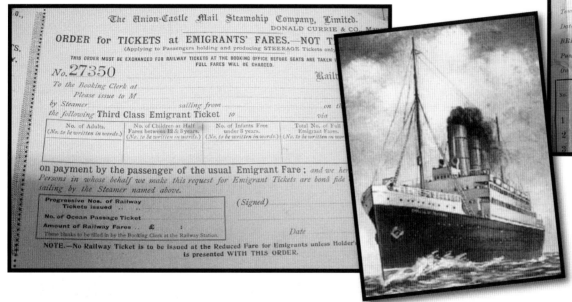

This is the Empress of Ireland, a ship which worked the emigrant trade across the Atlantic. Tragedy struck her when she was 'holed' by a Norwegian collier in fog on the St. Lawrence River. 1,012 people were drowned, 8 more than were lost on the Titanic.

One hundred years ago the steamships companies were competing with each other for emigrants' business. This display card shows how far you could travel into Canada with the White Star Line out of Belfast and through Canada on the railroad. Shipping agents were to be found in every town. This ticket is for a trans-atlantic crossing in March 1908 on the *California*, a passenger ship owned by the Hendersons Brothers' Anchor Line. Passengers were embarked at Moville, at the mouth of the Foyle. The *California* carried thousands of emigrants across the Atlantic. In June 1914 the ship, homeward bound, ran aground in heavy fog, on Tory Island. After being refloated she continued on the Atlantic trade until 1917 when a German torpedo sank her off the south-west of Ireland.

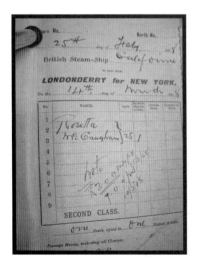

John Higgins from Dervock bought a ticket and left Donegal Quay, Belfast, in April 1911 on the *Lake Champlain* which belonged to the Canadian Pacific Railway Company Atlantic Steamship Lines. Six months later he sent home enough money for his fiancée, Sarah Scott from Drumawillan in Ballycastle, to join him. They married in Edmonton in 1911 and sent back the first photo of their new home a year later and another the next.

John had previously worked in America and South Africa in common with many other young men who had to seek work away from home.

How did he meet Sarah? Well, she worked in the post office across the street in Dervock from the Higgins' home. In this photo from an earlier voyage abroad, John is in the middle of the second row down below the guy with the cap.

Interestingly Sarah's mother was McCaughan from Stroanshesk. I wonder if she was related to Rosetta who's ticket is on a previous page?

In the 1920s emigrants were encouraged to move to Canada under the "Empire Settlement Scheme". This scheme provided land and ready-built homesteads for farming families.

Photographs of the families and their new homes in New Brunswick and Manitoba were printed in local publications to encourage others to join them.

Now many of their descendants return to us searching for their 'roots'. Hopefully this book has provided a glimpse of what their ancestors left behind them.

The emigrant's dream of home.